Roman Egypt: The History and Legacy of Ancient Egypt as a Province of Rome

By Charles River Editors

An ancient bust of Cleopatra VII, the last ruler of Egypt's Ptolemaic dynasty

About Charles River Editors

Charles River Editors is a boutique digital publishing company, specializing in bringing history back to life with educational and engaging books on a wide range of topics. Keep up to date with our new and free offerings with this 5 second sign up on our weekly mailing list, and visit Our Kindle Author Page to see other recently published Kindle titles.

We make these books for you and always want to know our readers' opinions, so we encourage you to leave reviews and look forward to publishing new and exciting titles each week.

Introduction

A baroque painting depicting the Battle of Actium

Roman Egypt

Africa may have given rise to the first human beings, and Egypt probably gave rise to the first great civilizations, which continue to fascinate modern societies across the globe nearly 5,000 years later. From the Library and Lighthouse of Alexandria to the Great Pyramid at Giza, the Ancient Egyptians produced several wonders of the world, revolutionized architecture and construction, created some of the world's first systems of mathematics and medicine, and established language and art that spread across the known world. With world-famous leaders like King Tut and Cleopatra, it's no wonder that today's world has so many Egyptologists.

What makes the accomplishments of the Ancient Egyptians all the more remarkable is that Egypt was historically a place of great political turbulence. Its position made it both valuable and vulnerable to tribes across the Mediterranean and the Middle East, and Ancient Egypt had no shortage of its own internecine warfare. Its most famous conquerors would come from Europe, with Alexander the Great laying the groundwork for the Hellenic Ptolemy line and the Romans extinguishing that line after defeating Cleopatra and driving her to suicide.

Perhaps the most intriguing aspect of ancient Egyptian civilization was its inception from the ground up, as the ancient Egyptians had no prior civilization which they could use as a template. In fact, ancient Egypt itself became a template for the civilizations that followed. The Greeks and the Romans were so impressed with Egyptian culture that they often attributed many attributes of their own culture–usually erroneously–to the Egyptians. With that said, some minor elements of ancient Egyptian culture were, indeed, passed on to later civilizations. Egyptian statuary appears to have had an initial influence on the Greek version, and the ancient Egyptian language continued long after the pharaonic period in the form of the Coptic language.

Although the Egyptians may not have passed their civilization directly on to later peoples, the key elements that comprised Egyptian civilization–their religion, early ideas of state, and art and architecture–can be seen in other pre-modern civilizations. For instance, civilizations far separated in time and space–such as China and Mesoamerica–possessed key elements that were similar to those found in ancient Egypt. Indeed, since Egyptian civilization represented some fundamental human concepts, a study of their culture can be useful when trying to understand many other pre-modern cultures.

Among all the periods in ancient Egyptian history, the Ptolemaic Kingdom and its most famous ruler, Cleopatra, may be the most well-known today. By the 4th century BCE, it appeared as though ancient Egypt was in its final death throes. It had long ceased to be an influential kingdom in the Near East and Mediterranean regions, and it had been ruled over by a succession of foreign peoples including Libyans, Nubians, Assyrians, and Persians. But just when Egypt seemed was doomed to pass forever into obscurity, it was reinvigorated by outsiders, most notably Alexander the Great. While in the process of campaigning to destroy the Achaemenid Persian Empire and conquer the world in 331 BCE, he made a pit stop in Egypt that forever changed the course of Egyptian history. Although his understanding of ancient Egyptian chronology and religion was minimal, Alexander was intrigued by ancient pharaonic culture, knowing, as the 5th century BCE Greek historian Herodotus once wrote, "Egypt is the gift of the Nile." As a result, Alexander endeavored to incorporate the land of the pharaohs into Hellenic Civilization.

Although Alexander never lived to rule over Egypt, one of his generals, Ptolemy I, did, and it was he who established the last great pharaonic dynasty in Egypt, known as the Ptolemaic Dynasty. The Ptolemies gave ancient Egypt an injection of vitality that had not been seen in the Nile Valley for centuries, preserving many aspects of native Egyptian culture while adding their own layer of Hellenic culture. The first few Ptolemaic rulers proved as able as any of their Egyptian predecessors as they worked to make Egypt a first-rate power in the world once again. Unfortunately, these able rulers were followed by a succession of corrupt and greedy kings, more concerned with personal wealth and power than the stability and greatness of their kingdom. Eventually, Ptolemaic Egypt collapsed due to weak rulers, internal social problems, and the rising power of Rome, but before the Ptolemaic Dynasty was extinguished, it proved to be one of the most impressive royal houses in ancient Egyptian history.

The end of the Ptolemies also happened to coincide with the most famous period of Roman history. In the latter 1st century BCE, men like Julius Caesar, Mark Antony, and Octavian participated in two civil wars that would spell the end of the Roman Republic and determine who would become the Roman emperor. In the middle of it all was history's most famous woman, Cleopatra, who famously seduced both Caesar and Antony and thereby positioned herself as one of the most influential people in a world of powerful men. Cleopatra was a legendary figure even to contemporary Romans and the ancient world, and she was a controversial figure who was equally reviled and praised through the years, depicted both as a benevolent ruler and an evil seductress (occasionally at the same time). Over 2,000 years after her death, everything about Cleopatra continues to fascinate people around the world, from her lineage as a Ptolemaic pharaoh, her physical features, the manner in which she seduced Caesar, her departure during the Battle of Actium, and her famous suicide. And despite being one of the most famous figures in history, there is still much mystery surrounding her and the end of the Ptolemies, leading historians and archaeologists scouring Alexandria, Egypt for clues about her life and Egypt's transition to Roman rule.

As for Roman Egypt, the period from 30 B.C. until the Roman Empire was split into two halves in the 4th century CE. It is scarcely mentioned, yet, it was a time when Egypt, if no longer a great power in its own right, was a pivotal province in the Roman Empire. It could also be argued it was a power without which the Roman Empire would not have survived. Its wealth, especially its fertility, was the key for any Roman emperor hoping to feed and entertain Rome's ever-demanding masses and was particularly vital to Augustus as he established himself as the first emperor of Egypt. The institution of imperial, as opposed to senatorial, provinces proved crucial in the consolidation of imperial power. Moreover, how Egypt in this period was administered and exploited provides invaluable information as to how Rome manipulated and controlled large populations for its benefit in the rest of its empire. Tactics used again and again throughout the Roman world were honed in this, the most valuable of Rome's provinces.

Egypt's key role in imperial politics was crucial, but so was its role in the rise of Christianity. For many years, the belief that Christianity had spread from Jerusalem to engulf the Roman Empire has been largely unchallenged, but more recent scholarship suggests the codification of Christian doctrine and success of missionaries from Alexandria and not Jerusalem, were instrumental in Christianity becoming the state religion of the empire. Given the importance of Christianity to both European and world history, this issue is of a real significance.

Roman Egypt: The History and Legacy of Ancient Egypt as a Province of Rome chronicles the tumultuous history of Egypt at the end of the 1st century BCE, and its role as a Roman province. Along with pictures depicting important people, places, and events, you will learn about Roman Egypt like never before.

Roman Egypt: The History and Legacy of Ancient Egypt as a Province of Rome
About Charles River Editors
Introduction
   The Collapse of the Egyptian Empire
   Incorporating Egypt as a Province
   The Prefects
   Christianity in Egypt
   Egypt and the Politics of the Empire
   Online Resources
   Bibliography
Free Books by Charles River Editors
Discounted Books by Charles River Editors

The Collapse of the Egyptian Empire

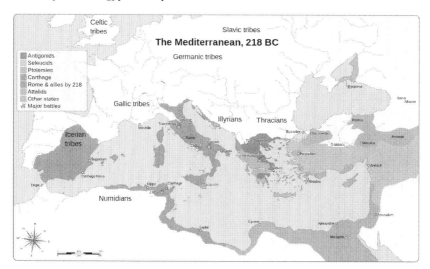

Goran Tek-en's map of the ancient empires in the Mediterranean in the late 3rd century BCE

By the end of the 1st century BCE, the Ptolemies had transformed Alexandria into the greatest city on the planet, and in many ways, the city proved to be immortal. But while Alexandria is still an important center in the eastern Mediterranean, the dynasty that built it saw its prospects quickly decline.

The decline of the dynasty and the constant troubles that plagued it can be traced to the rule of Ptolemy IV Philopator (221-204 BCE). The Ptolemies became too concerned with taking small tracts of land from the Seleucids in Coele-Syria while Rome became the preeminent power in the Mediterranean, and the most impressive achievement of Ptolemy IV was his victory over the Seleucid King Antiochus III (241-187 BCE) in the Fourth Syrian War, during which the Seleucids pursued a campaign to wrest back Coele-Syria from the Ptolemies that culminated in a battle near the city of Raphia. Strabo explained, "After Gaza one comes to Rhaphia, where a battle was fought between Ptolemaeus the Fourth and Antiochus the Great" (Strabo, *Geography*, XVI, 2, 31). The result was a victory for Ptolemy IV, but it proved to be ephemeral since a rebellion of native Egyptians had begun in Upper Egypt.

After Ptolemy IV's death, the instability inherent in his reign turned into a succession crisis, during which native Egyptian priests temporarily ruled in the south and a minor noble ruled in Alexandria (Chauveau 2000, 11). Stability was finally reestablished by the young Ptolemy V

Epiphanes (204-181 BCE) in 186 BCE. Ptolemy V is best known for marrying one of Antiochus III's daughters, Cleopatra I—the first royal Ptolemy woman of seven to take the now famous name—which brought temporary peace to the warring Ptolemies and Seleucids.

Although Ptolemy V reestablished order within Egypt's borders, others were waiting outside the gates for a chance to attack. The situation between the Ptolemies and Seleucids took another turn after Ptolemy V died and was succeeded by Ptolemy VI Philometer (180-145 BCE), who spent most of his reign dealing with rebellious elements in the Alexandrian court. Sensing weakness in Egypt, the Seleucid King Antiochus IV (175-164 BCE) attacked Egypt's possessions in Coele-Syria in 169 BCE (Chauveau 2000, 13). The campaign was a stunning success for the Seleucids, who drove their forces deep into Egypt, where Antiochus IV had himself proclaimed pharaoh in the traditional capital of Memphis (Chauveau 2000, 13).

Throughout this, Ptolemy VI was more concerned with fighting his brother Ptolemy VIII Euregetes II (170-163 and again in 145-116). Antiochus supported Ptolemy VIII but was ultimately rebuffed by the Romans, who knew that a civil war in Egypt would be bad for their economy because that was where they got much of their grain. They also were not keen to see either the Seleucids or Ptolemies acquire too much power in the eastern Mediterranean.

For those reasons, the Roman Senate decided to take Ptolemy VI's side and gave Antiochus IV an ultimatum. The 3rd century CE Roman historian Cassius Dio explained, "Ptolemy, the ruler of Egypt, passed away leaving two sons and one daughter. When the brothers began to quarrel with each other about the sovereignty, Antiochus, the son of Antiochus the Great, sheltered the younger, who had been driven out, in order that under the pretext of defending him he might get his hands on Egyptian affairs. In a campaign directed against Egypt he conquered the greater part of the country and spent some time in besieging Alexandria. When the rest sought refuge with the Romans, Popilius was sent to Antiochus and bade him keep his hands off Egypt; for the brothers, comprehending the designs of Antiochus, had become reconciled. When the latter was for putting off his reply, Popilius drew a circle about him with his staff and demanded that he deliberate and answer standing where he was. Antiochus then in fear raised the siege." (Cassius Dio, *Roman History*, XX, 9, 25)

Roman intervention in the sixth and final Syrian War was a sign of things to come. Although the Greek kingdoms had long been the preeminent powers in the region, the upstart Romans now used a combination of their military might and diplomacy to shape the Mediterranean. After the Romans had wielded their might, the Seleucids focused their attention on reacquiring possessions they had lost in Coele-Syria, while Ptolemaic Egypt continued to decline.

While the young Ptolemy VI was on the throne, he had to contend with his older brother, Ptolemy VIII Euergetes II, who continued trying to replace him. Ptolemy VIII was temporarily successful and briefly ruled during the Sixth Syrian War, but he was deposed and exiled to the colony of Cyrene. Fate stepped in once more to give Ptolemy VIII a reprieve when his brother died and he was recalled to Alexandria.

Among the Ptolemaic kings, Ptolemy VIII would probably be the closest to one what thinks of as a stereotypical ancient despot. Unlike most of his predecessors, who had colorful nicknames—some of which are translated into English as "savior" (soter) or "flutist" (auletes)—Ptolemy VIII was given the moniker of "physkon," or "fat." Unlike the first three Ptolemies, Physkon was no patron of the arts, and despite being known for his weight, he was also notoriously thin-skinned. Instead of building on the accomplishments of his illustrious predecessors, Physkon spent most of his time going after his political enemies and those who had offended him. One of his most notable targets was the famed Library of Alexandria, home to many prominent free thinkers of the time. Once he learned that a fair amount of opposition had originated in the halls of the Library, he closed the institution's doors for the remainder of his rule (Chauveau 2000, 15). An example of the tactics Physkon used to suppress opposition was recorded by Strabo. "But after this mass of people had also been blotted out, chiefly by Euergetes Physcon, in whose time Polybius went to Alexandria (for, being opposed by factions, Physcon more often sent the masses against the soldiers and thus caused their destruction)." (Strabo, *Geography*, XVII, I, 12).

Ptolemy XII came to power after Ptolemy XI Alexander II (who only ruled for a few days in 80 BCE) killed his wife and incurred the wrath of an Alexandrian mob, losing his life in the process (Chauveau 2000, 18). Besides being the father of Cleopatra VII, Ptolemy XII was known for his pursuit of the arts and humanities, earning the nickname the "flutist" in the process, but in terms of imperial policy, Ptolemy XII was weak and ineffective, and he nearly destroyed the Egyptian economy when he devalued the currency (Chauveau 2000, 22).

Ptolemy XII's accession to the throne was marked by plotting and bribery on a grand scale, and once he was in place he grew so paranoid that, suspicious of his provincial governors, he insisted on concentrating almost all executive powers in Alexandria, where he had his seat. Such a system of government could not hope to cope with, or indeed understand, the problems faced by the Egyptian kingdom's most far-spread provinces, and inevitably there were violent uprisings by those subjects at the borders of the kingdom who felt themselves abandoned to their fate. Cyprus and Cyrenaica were both lost, and other rebellions were crushed only with great difficulty and expense. At this time, Egypt had effectively become a client state of Rome – and a valued trading asset, as they provided the majority of grain imports to the capital – and, in 58 BCE, despite unrest at home, Ptolemy was obliged to travel to Rome on an official visit. He chose to take Cleopatra, then just a child, with him as well, but what was meant to be a short trip ended up becoming a three-year exile. Taking advantage of his absence, another Cleopatra seized the throne.

It is unclear which Cleopatra this was, as records from the period are sparse and not helped by the fact that the Ptolemies favored re-using the same names over and over again. She may either have been Cleopatra V, making her Cleopatra VII's mother, or Cleopatra VI, which would mean she was a sister. Either way, this Cleopatra's reign was to be short-lived, because within a few months of her accession to the throne, she died suddenly under mysterious circumstances. It is highly likely that she was murdered, most probably at the hand of Berenice IV, Cleopatra VII's older sister, who took the throne as soon as she died. Berenice reigned for just under three years in Alexandria, until Ptolemy XII finally returned at the head of a Roman army led by General Aulus Gabinius. Ptolemy had been forced to go hat in hand to Rome, having virtually no support outside of Alexandria and no chance of regaining his throne by raising armies of his own. Though this move allowed Ptolemy to recapture the throne of Egypt, he had effectively made his kingdom a vassal state of Rome, garrisoned by Roman armies, propped up by Roman spears, and dependent on Roman goodwill.

Betrayed by at least one of his eldest daughters, if not two (or his wife), Ptolemy XII seems to have turned to Cleopatra VII, his companion during his three-year exile, as his sole repository of trust. At age 14, he proclaimed her regent, a largely ceremonial position which nonetheless placed her in direct line to the throne in the event of his death. Ptolemy's reign limped on for another four years, amid further losses of crucial territory and an ever-growing dependence on Gabinius's troops, whose officers had established themselves – apparently permanently – in Egypt and promptly formed their own political faction, the *Gabiniani*, in order to try and carve themselves their own piece of the rich Egyptian pie.

Finally, in 51 BCE, Ptolemy XII died, leaving an 18-year-old Cleopatra at a crossroads. She could not assume sole rulership, for such an act would require her to get rid of her younger brother, Ptolemy XIII, with whom she was expected to share power. Cleopatra was also, in keeping with dynastic tradition, required to marry Ptolemy XIII, who was 10 years old at the time. With the weight of tradition upon her, Cleopatra complied, but it would certainly not be a happy union. The two seem not to have gotten along as brother and sister, never mind as husband and wife, and their joint rule was marked by more uprisings. To add insult to injury, the Nile stubbornly refused to deliver adequate floods. Egypt's fertile grain fields were dependent on the periodic flooding of the Nile basin, which would coat the fields with a natural fertilizer, and a sparse flood meant even sparser harvests, which meant not only that the people would go hungry but that Egypt would be unable to deliver sufficient grain to Rome, with all the perilous consequences that entailed.

Just a few months after ascending to the throne, Cleopatra effectively divorced her younger brother, whose influence was limited by his age. She no longer appeared with him at official ceremonies, and started being the sole signatory on official documents, a gross breach of tradition. In Ptolemaic tradition, female co-rulers were technically subordinate to their male counterparts, regardless of whether this was actually the case, so doing away with Ptolemy was a slap in the face to the many traditionalists at court. Having made enemies of the traditionalists, she promptly followed this political mistake in 50 BCE by upsetting one of the most powerful political factions in Egypt, the *Gabiniani*. Having been in Egypt for approximately five years, the *Gabiniani* had essentially severed their ties to Rome.

When some exponents of the *Gabiniani* murdered the sons of Marcus Bibulus, the governor of Syria, who had been sent in friendship to request their aid in a military campaign against the neighbouring Parthians, Cleopatra saw a chance to intervene and cut the *Gabiniani* down to size. She had the assassins seized, put in chains, and delivered to Bibulus, but while this may have curried favour with the Roman governor, it did nothing to endear her to the *Gabiniani*, who promptly went from uneasy allies to sworn enemies. Cleopatra could hardly hope to rule long in the face of such massed political hostility, and in 48 BC, a plot spearheaded by Pothinus, a eunuch in the palace service, with the collusion of Cleopatra's many enemies, forced her from the throne and placed the more biddable, pliant Ptolemy XIII on it as sole ruler of Egypt. Cleopatra now found herself a fugitive.

Cleopatra VII was exiled to Upper Egypt and then fled to Palestine in order to escape a potential assassination, and at some point during this time, she made contact with Julius Caesar in order to elicit his support for her claim to the Egyptian throne. At the time, Rome was tearing itself apart, and the repercussions of this conflict were being felt across the Mediterranean. Caesar, former consul and governor of Gaul, had marched across the Rubicon, illegally bringing his armies onto Italian soil and threatening Rome itself, with the purpose of making himself dictator. Caesar was opposed by his former ally, the once-great general Pompey Magnus. By this time, Pompey was an old, spent man, while Caesar was still vigorous, and Caesar had chased Pompey's army from Rome, hounded it all the way to southern Italy, and then, when Pompey escaped across the Mediterranean to Greece, he had loaded his army onto a fleet and shipped it across the sea, where he had annihilated Pompey's armies at Pharsalus in 48 BCE.

Pompey barely escaped with his life, and virtually alone and penniless, he had taken ship for Egypt, where he arrived as a supplicant, possibly hoping for military assistance from the *Gabiniani,* or from Ptolemy XIII himself. Having heard a rumor that Pompey was attempting to raise men against him in Egypt, Caesar took ship for Alexandria, only to find upon his arrival that Pompey had been murdered on the orders of Egypt's young pharaoh, the boy-king Ptolemy XIII. Possibly encouraged by Pothinus, Ptolemy had Pompey Magnus put to death almost immediately after his arrival in Egypt, the end result apparently being that he hoped to ingratiate himself with Caesar, whose victory at Pharsalus had, by default, made him the uncontested ruler of Rome and thus the most powerful man in the known world.

An ancient bust of Pompey

Ptolemy XIII, however, had completely misunderstood Caesar. When the Roman general arrived in Egypt a bare two days later, hot on Pompey's heels, Ptolemy XIII received Caesar with great pomp and presented him with Pompey's head. Pompey had been a close friend of Caesar's before their rivalry spiraled out of control, and had even married Caesar's daughter, who had died in childbirth before the war.

The year was 48 BCE, and Rome's strongest man was now in Egypt and positioned to decide who would rule. Dio noted, "Cleopatra, it seems, had at first urged with Caesar her claim against her brother by means of agents, but as soon as she discovered his disposition (which was very susceptible, to such an extent that he had his intrigues with ever so many other women—with all, doubtless, who chance to come in his way) she sent word to him that she was being betrayed by her friends and asked that she be allowed to plead her case in person…She asked therefore for admission to his presence, and on obtaining permission adorned and beautified herself so as to appear before him in the most majestic and at the same time pity-inspiring guise…Afterward he entered an assembly of theirs, and producing Ptolemy and Cleopatra, read their father's will, in which it was directed that they should live together according to the custom of the Egyptians and rule in common, and that the Roman people should exercise a guardianship over them." (Cassius Dio, *Roman History*, XLII, 34-35)

The peace did not last very long, and Caesar had to demonstrate his martial abilities to the supporters of Ptolemy XIII in no time. According to Caesar's own account, taking the Pharos Island—where the Lighthouse had been located—was crucial for taking and holding Alexandria. He wrote, "On the island there is a tower called Pharos, of great height, a work of wonderful construction, which took its name from the island. This island, lying over against Alexandria, makes a harbor [sic], but it is connected with the town by a narrow roadway like a bridge, piers nine hundred feet in length having been thrown out seawards by former kings. On this island there are dwelling-houses of Egyptians and a settlement the size of a town, and any ships that went a little out of their course there through carelessness or rough weather they were in the habit of plundering like pirates. Moreover, on account of the narrowness of the passage there can be no entry for ships into the harbour [sic] without the consent of those who are in occupation of Pharos. Caesar, now fearing such difficulty, landed his troops when the enemy was occupied in fighting, and seized Pharos and placed a garrison on it. The result of these measures was that corn and reinforcements could be safely conveyed to him on shipboard." (Julius Caesar, *The Civil Wars*, III, 112).

Gautier Poupeau's picture of a bust of Caesar

After Caesar had won the Egyptian civil war for Cleopatra, he demonstrated his diplomatic abilities by bringing the two factions back together. Since Ptolemy XIII had died in his attempted escape from Caesar's clutches, the Roman general ordered that Cleopatra "marry" her other brother in a very Ptolemaic-style wedding. Dio explained, "In this way Caesar overcame Egypt. He did not, however, make it subject to the Romans, but bestowed it upon Cleopatra, for whose sake he had waged the conflict. Yet, being afraid that the Egyptians might rebel again, because they were delivered over to a woman to rule, and that the Romans might be angry, both on this account and because he was living with the woman, he commanded her to "marty" her other brother, and gave the kingdom to both to them, at least nominally. For in reality Cleopatra was to hold all the power alone, since her husband was still a boy, and in view of Caesar's favour [sic] there was nothing that she could not do. Hence her living with her brother and sharing the rule with him was a mere pretence [sic] which she accepted, whereas in truth she ruled alone and spent her time in Caesar's company." (Cassius Dio, *Roman History*, XLII, 44)

After assuring the situation in Alexandria was stable once more, Caesar returned to Rome, where he was proclaimed "dictator for life." He did, however, leave Cleopatra with more than one gift. From 47-30 BCE, Cleopatra VII would rule Egypt as sole monarch, but unfortunately few documents, either Greek or Egyptian, exist that can shed more details on her rule (Chauveau 2000, 24). Cleopatra gave birth to Caesar's son—whom she named Ptolemy Caesar—on July 23, 47 BCE. She then traveled to Rome with her son three years later and was in the Eternal City when Caesar was assassinated by the Senate on March 15, 44 BCE, the Ides of March (Chauveau 2000, 25).

The assassination sparked a new round in the civil wars, pitting the Senate against the Second Triumvirate of Octavian, Mark Antony, and Lepidus. Once the triumvirate won the war, Cleopatra sided with them and developed a close personal relationship with Mark Antony.

Antony

As per the agreement between Antony, Octavian, and Lepidus, Antony was given control of

Rome's eastern provinces, which included Egypt, although it was still nominally independent. In 37 BCE, Antony and Cleopatra began their infamous affair, which saw the Roman general adopt more and more Hellenistic and Egyptian styles and nomenclature, much to his reputation's detriment back in Rome (Chauveau 2000, 27).

As Antony and Cleopatra struggled with unrest in the east, back in Rome Octavian had dismissed Lepidus, the third member of the Second Triumvirate, and assumed sole power over his domains, while also continuing a vigorous smear campaign against Antony. Octavian denounced him for abandoning his wife Octavia and his children, and he accused Antony of going native with his wanton Egyptian queen. Octavian's public relations offensive blamed Antony's recent failure and the consequent loss of Roman life on the wrath of the gods for Antony's sins.

An ancient bust of Octavian

Antony and Cleopatra, however, seem to have been unconcerned with Octavian's threats, or the growing popular resentment with Antony that Octavian was fomenting in Rome. It seems quite likely that Antony simply did not care anymore and just wanted to be left alone in his Alexandrian idyll with the woman he loved. Like Caesar, Antony was fully charmed by the quixotic and exotic Egyptian lifestyle, and he immersed himself in it even more than his famous mentor. Despite repeated demands from Octavian that he return to Rome immediately to answer for his conduct, Antony remained happily in Alexandria, and instead waged a new campaign against the Armenians in 34 BCE, this time achieving success and annexing the territory to his and Cleopatra's domains.

It was in the aftermath of this war that Cleopatra and Antony finally overstepped their mark. Cleopatra organised a lavish, Roman-style Triumph in Alexandria to mark Antony's successful conquest, during which Antony's children (now numbering three) by Cleopatra were all granted royal titles in the East, Cleopatra herself was named Queen of Queens and ruler of the East, and crucially, Cleopatra's son Caesarion was named King of Kings, ruler of Egypt and the East, living God, and above all – Caesar's formal sole son and heir, thereby by default disowning Octavian in the eyes of the East. Additionally, Antony officially declared his alliance with Octavian over, proclaiming that from then on the East was free and independent of Rome. It was the biggest blunder of their lives.

In 32 BCE, Octavian declared war against Cleopatra, not Antony, a calculated move intended to ensure the Romans did not feel he was continuing the legacy of the fratricidal civil war. Perhaps Octavian overestimated his support, for Cleopatra and Antony were delighted to discover that both consuls and a full third of the Senate had decamped from Rome and defected to their side wholesale. The royal couple met the defectors in Greece, and for a while felt so secure in their position they even considered an invasion of Italy itself.

Their victory was to prove short-lived, however. In 31 BCE, Octavian's forces set sail for Greece, and the legions there immediately went over to his side, spurred by the veterans in their ranks who had once fought for his adoptive father Caesar. Both Cyrenaica and Greece fell to Octavian, essentially without a blow struck, and Cleopatra and Antony were forced to retreat back to Egypt, where they rallied the Eastern navies and prepared to contest Octavian's passage across the Mediterranean.

On September 2, 31 BCE, Antony and Cleopatra found themselves in a tactically disadvantageous position, facing Octavian's navies off the coast of Actium, in Greece. With the risk of being bottled up and surrounded at Actium by Octavian's naval forces a very real possibility, Cleopatra advised Antony to give battle, although it appears the Roman general thought victory was an unlikely possibility. Antony and Cleopatra appeared, to the untrained eye, to have the advantage: their fleet numbered over 500 vessels, almost half of which were giant five-decked quinquiremes, ramming warships that carried full-blown siege engines on board, while Octavian had only 250 far lighter craft.

However, the sea was rough that morning, favoring Octavian's more maneuverable ships, which were less affected by the rolling swells, and to make matters worse, Antony's fleet had been wracked by disease, meaning that many of his mighty quinquiremes were undermanned. The giant craft were ponderous to begin with, but without the requisite number of rowers and fighting men, they could never hope to achieve proper ramming speed. Octavian's lighter, more agile craft, filled with veteran sailors, were able to dance around the ponderous quinquiremes, showering them with hails of fire arrows, ramming and boarding where they could, and sprinting away before the heavier craft had a chance to bring their rams to bear. As the day wore on, it became more and more apparent to Antony and Cleopatra, on their twin flagships, that the battle would be lost. More and more of their craft were being sunk, scattered or overwhelmed, and still more were burning down to the waterline, their skeleton crews being insufficient to man their battle stations and extinguish fires at the same time. As night approached, Antony and Cleopatra spotted a gap in the now thoroughly jumbled enemy line, and ordered their ships to speed through it without delay, making for Alexandria with all speed and abandoning their entire navy to its fate. It was a crushing blow, for Octavian and his generals had virtually annihilated Egypt's seaborne power.

As one of Rome's most famous battles, and one of the most famous events in Cleopatra's life, the Battle of Actium has taken on a life of its own in popular memory. One of the longest-held myths about the battle is that Cleopatra, sensing defeat, began to sail away from the fight in the middle of the day, and the lovestruck Antony followed her with his own ship, abandoning his men in the middle of the fight. While that popular myth would be in keeping with explaining Cleopatra's irresistible charm and magnetism, contemporary accounts of the battle do not suggest it was actually the case.

Once the Battle of Actium was over, Mark Antony and Cleopatra were forced to flee back to Egypt. Dio wrote, "At the time he sent a part of the fleet in pursuit of Antony and Cleopatra; these ships, accordingly, followed after the fugitives, but when it became clear that they were not going to overtake them, they returned. With his remaining vessels he capture the enemy's entrenchments, meeting with no opposition because of their small numbers, and then overtook and without a battle won over the rest of the army, which was retreating to Macedonia." (Cassius Dio, *Roman History*, LI, 1, 4).

After the loss at Actium, it was just a matter of time before Octavian caught up with Antony and Cleopatra. According to Dio, Antony attempted to enlist the help of some of his former allies in North Africa who had rebuffed his advances, before concentrating his energies on the defense of Alexandria. Dio explained, "Now among the other preparations they made for speedy warfare, they enrolled among the youths of military age, Cleopatra her son Caesarion and Antony [and] his son Antyllus, who had been born to him by Fulvia and was then with him. Their purpose was to arouse the enthusiasm of the Egyptians, who would feel that they had at last a man for their king, and to cause the rest to continue the struggle with these boys as their leaders, in case anything untoward should happen to the parents." (Cassius Dio, *Roman History*, LI, 6, 1-2)

While preparations for the defense of Alexandria were being made by Antony, Cleopatra once more demonstrated how she had reached the pinnacle of Ptolemaic power by sending overtures to Octavian behind Antony's back: "Meanwhile Cleopatra, on her part, unknown to Antony, sent to him a golden scepter and a golden crown together with the royal throne, signifying that through them she offered him the kingdom as well; for she hoped that even if he did hate Antony, he would yet take pity on her at least. Caesar accepted her gifts as a good omen, but made no answer to Antony; to Cleopatra, however, although he publicly sent threatening messages, including the announcement that, if she would give up her armed forces and renounce her sovereignty, he would consider what ought to be done in her case, he secretly sent word that, if she would kill Antony, he would grant her pardon and leave her realm inviolate." (Cassius Dio, *Roman History*, LI, 6, 5-6)

The end was near for the lovers, but the classical sources disputed the details of their legendary deaths. Of all the fictionalized portrayals of Cleopatra VII's rise and fall, perhaps the most memorable scenes involve her and Antony's deaths. Once again, Dio provided the most detailed account of the events. According to him, after Antony had lost a pivotal battle to Octavian near the Egyptian Delta city of Pelusium, Antony attempted to flee, but he was tricked by Cleopatra into believing that she was dead, the purpose being that she would subsequently conclude a peace deal with Octavian. Dio wrote, "After his unexpected setback, Antony took refuge in his fleet, and was preparing to give battle on the sea or at any rate to sail to Spain. But Cleopatra, upon perceiving this, caused the ships to desert, and she herself rushed suddenly into the mausoleum, pretending that she feared Caesar and desired by some means or other to forestall him by taking her own life, but really as an invitation to Antony to enter there also. He had a suspicion, to be sure, that he was being betrayed, yet in his infatuation he could not believe it, but actually pitied her more, one might say, than himself. Cleopatra, doubtless, was fully aware of this and hoped that if he should be informed that she was dead, he would not wish to survive her, but would die at once...He first asked one of the bystanders to slay him; but when the man drew his sword and slew himself, Antony wished to imitate his courage and so gave himself a wound and fell upon his face, causing the bystanders to believe that he was dead...Now when some of them saw her peering out at this point, they raised a shout so that even Antony heard. So he, learning that she survived, stood up, as if he had still the power to live; but, as he had lost much blood, he despaired of his life and besought the bystanders to carry him to the monument and to hoist him up by the ropes that were hanging there to life the stone blocks." (Cassius Dio, *Roman History*, LI, 10, 5-9)

Cleopatra then tried to save her own life - and possibly her position as regent of Egypt - by negotiating with Octavian, but the future emperor wanted to bring her back alive to Rome, where he would presumably parade her through the streets during his triumph and then ritually strangle her. Once Cleopatra realized the ramifications of Octavian's plans for her, she made the decision to commit suicide.

The manner of Cleopatra's death has been debated for millennia, shaped in popular memory by everyone from Shakespeare to Hollywood. Ancient historians wrote that she had a venomous snake, most likely a cobra, concealed in her private apartments, and that when she realised that escape was impossible, she provoked it into administering a fatal bite on her arm. Today most people unfamiliar with those accounts believe that Cleopatra had an asp bite her on the breast, which was how Shakespeare depicted it in his famous play. Stories differ as to what snake was used (the term "asp" is most likely a generic name for any venomous snake, but Egypt is renowned for its deadly King Cobra) and if it was kept deliberately or came to be there by accident. Some historians even argue that there was no snake at all, and that Cleopatra poisoned herself with hemlock, as Socrates had done. Still others claim Octavian had her killed, which seems contrary to the widely-assumed belief that Octavian intended to parade her as a captive through the streets of Rome in a triumph.

Although people are now familiar with the venomous snake bite version, Dio was adamant the method of death she had chosen for herself is unknown. "But when she could accomplish nothing, she feigned a change of heart, pretending to set great hopes in him and also in Livia. She said she would sail of her own free will, and she made ready some treasured articles of adornment to use as gifts, in the hope that by these means she might inspire belief that it was not her purpose to die, and so might be less closely guarded and thus be able to destroy herself…She put on her most beautiful apparel, arranged her body in most seemingly fashion, took in her hands all the emblems of royalty, and so died. No one knows clearly in what way she perished, for the only marks on her body were slight pricks on the arm." (Cassius Dio, *Roman History*, LI, 13-14, 1).

Although Dio's account of Cleopatra's death is probably the most detailed, Strabo, who was a contemporary of Cleopatra's, declared it had been an asp that had killed the queen. "Having passed through the Hippodrome, one comes to Nicopolis, which has a settlement on the sea no smaller than a city. It is thirty stadia distant from Alexandria. Augustus Caesar honoured [sic] this place because it was here that the conquered in battle those who came out against him with Antony; and when he had taken the city at the first onset, he forced Antony to put himself to death and Cleopatra came into his power alive; but a little later she too put herself to death secretly, while in prison, by the bite of an asp or (for two accounts are given) by applying a poisonous ointment; and the result was that the empire of the sons of Lagus, which had endured for many years, was dissolved." (Strabo, *Geography*, XVII, I, 10)

Regardless of how it happened, Cleopatra's death marked the end of Egyptian independence. Egypt became a province of Rome, but that did not necessarily mean the Ptolemaic Dynasty was finished. Although Octavian was never known as a military genius, he was adept in many other respects, especially when it concerned the art of politics and the ability to see things in the long-term. Octavian knew that even with Cleopatra VII dead, her children, especially Caesarion, might claim the throne of Egypt, and Octavian could not let that happen. Dio explained, "Such were these two and such was their end. Of their children, Antyllus was slain immediately, though he was betrothed to the daughter of Caesar and had taken refuge in his father's shrine, which Cleopatra had built; and Caesarian while fleeing to Ethiopia was overtaken on the road and murdered." (Cassius Dio, *Roman History*, LI, 15, 5).

Incorporating Egypt as a Province

Once his conquest was complete and all potential rivals were exterminated, Octavian immediately set to work incorporating Egypt into the Roman Empire. The nuances of the transition of power from the Ptolemies to the Roman empire were described by Dio as follows: "In the case of the Egyptians and Alexandrians, he spared them all, so that none perished. The truth was that he did not see fit to inflict any irreparable injury upon a people so numerous, who might prove very useful to the Romans in many ways; nevertheless, he offered as a pretext for his kindness their god Serapis, their founder Alexander, and, in the third place, their fellow-citizen Areius, of whose learning and companionship he availed himself. The speech in which he proclaimed to them his pardon he delivered in Greek, so that they might understand him. After this he viewed the body of Alexander and actually touched it, whereupon, it is said, a piece of the nose was broken off. But he declined to view the remains of the Ptolemies, though the Alexandrians were extremely eager to show them, remarking, "I wished to see a king, not corpses." For this same reason he would not enter the presence of Apis, either declaring that he was accustomed to worship gods, not cattle…For in view of the populousness of both the cities and country, the facile, fickle character of the inhabitants, and the extent of the grain-supply and of the wealth, so far from daring to entrust the land to any senator, he would not even grant a senator permission to live in it, except as he personally made the concession to him by name. On the other hand he did not allow the Egyptians to be senators in Rome…Thus was Egypt enslaved. All the inhabitants who resisted for a time were finally subdued, as, indeed, Heaven very clearly indicated to them beforehand." (Cassius Dio, *Roman History*, LI, 16, 3-17, 4).

Augustus' domination of Rome was largely achieved through patronage dependent upon his control of Egypt, which he exercised through the equestrian class rather than the traditional senatorial families. Senators had to apply for special permission to visit the province. The prefects he personally appointed had unrestricted independent jurisdiction. In the system introduced by Augustus and maintained with minor changes by his successors, the prefect was at the top of the governmental tree followed by the *juridicus*, also someone appointed from the equestrian class and directly appointed by the princeps himself. This office holder had judicial power over all of Egypt. The *archdicasres*, chief judge, came next in the hierarchy, though he was not actually a judge but rather, an official linked to Alexandria, usually from one of Rome's leading families. He had control of debt collecting and the Public Record Office, as well as anything connected to Alexandria. The next in seniority was the *idiologus*, who was the financial officer in charge of the *idios logos*, or special account, for Egypt. This account included the more irregular or uncertain sources of income, such as fines and confiscations.

Strabo praised the system initiated by Augustus for the governance of the Egypt: "Egypt is now a Province and it not only pays considerable tribute but also is governed by prudent men, the prefects who are sent there from time to time. Now he who is sent has the rank of the king and subordinate to him is the administrator of justice who has supreme authority over most of the law suits and another is the official called Idiologus who enquires into all properties that are without owners and that ought to fall to Caesar and these are attended by freedmen of Caesar as also by stewards who are entrusted with affairs of more or less importance."[1]

Augustus was always aware of the importance of the army in maintaining control, and he paid particular attention to Egypt in this regard. Strabo describes the force garrisoned in the new province: "There are three legions of soldiers, one of which is stationed in the city and the others in the country. Apart from these there are nine Roman cohorts, three in the city, three on the borders of Ethiopia in Syene as a guard for that region, and three in the rest of the country. There are also three bodies of cavalry, which likewise are assigned to the critical points."[2]

A flotilla of ships was also stationed on the Nile, making Egypt the most militarized of all Roman provinces. While initiating a supervising administrative authority, Augustus utilized much of the administrative system set up by the Ptolemies, and Strabo confirms this policy: "Of the native officials in the city one is the Interpreter who is clad in purple, has hereditary prerogatives and has charge of the interests of the city and another, the Recorder, and another the Night Commander. Now these officers existed also in the time of the kings but since the kings were carrying on a bad government the prosperity of the city was also vanishing on account of the prevalent lawlessness."[3]

Officials called e*pistrategi, nomarchs,* and *ethnarchs* were appointed throughout Egypt to oversee a whole range of issues relating to daily life, as had been the case in the time of the Ptolemies. Polybius, who had visited Alexandria, described it as being inhabited by three distinct classes. The first was the Egyptians, whom he characterized as quick-tempered and disinclined to what he termed civic life. The next was the mercenary class, whom he believed was "severe, numerous and intractable."[4] The final class was the Alexandrians, whom he had a similarly poor opinion of their potential for civil life as he did of the Egyptians, but grudgingly conceded they were better than the others. From his perspective, being Greek—or at least, partly Greek—meant they had some veneer of Hellenistic civilization.

The Prefects

As an imperial province rather than a senatorial province, Egypt was always governed on the emperors' behalf by prefects, a total of 110 of them, until the empire split centuries later. The normal period of rule was a maximum of four years, but the time served often depended on factors such as changing emperors or assessments of success or failure. The prefects were all drawn from the equestrian class, a group that Augustus quite consciously promoted as a counter to the Senate. These knights, as they are sometimes called because of their association with

---

[1] Strabo, *Geography*, 17.1.12.
[2] Strabo, *Geography*, 17.1.12.
[3] Strabo, *Geography*, 17.1.12.
[4] Strabo, *Geography*, 17.1.12

horses, were the second rank in Roman society after the senatorial class. The rank was passed from father to son, but each *eques* had to meet the property threshold at the five year census. The property threshold was approximately 50,000 denarii in the Republican period, but this was doubled by Augustus.

During the reign of Augustus *equites* came to fill the senior administrative and military positions within the empire. The most senior were reserved for the senatorial class, but the two most powerful positions to which a member of the equestrian class could aspire were prefect of the Praetorians and prefect of Egypt. There was a degree of similarity between the normal careers of those in the top two tiers of Roman society. A young Roman in those classes would usually start his career in a number of junior administrative positions in Rome or Italy. This would be followed by about 10 years of military service as an officer, and then, assuming all had gone reasonably well, he would take on senior administrative or military position in the provinces.

The two classes combined never reached more than approximately 10,000 in number in an empire with a population of between 50 and 70 million, but this small group dominated political and military power and tended to monopolize economic power in different ways. The strictures on members of the senatorial class indulging in trade meant they tended to concentrate on the acquisition of land while the equestrians, although owning large estates, dominated trade, shipping, mining, and manufacturing.[5] In the Roman system, the tax-farming companies, which were so lucrative, were almost monopolized by *equites*.

The number of senators was restricted to 600 under Augustus and was maintained at this level until 312 CE. The sons of senators held the equestrian rank until they were given a senatorial seat, but Augustus initiated a fundamental change in the system by altering a number of key elements regarding who could become a senator and who would be accorded equestrian status. These included raising the property qualification for membership of the Senate to 250,000 denarii, and as already noted, *equites* to 100,000 denarii. His aim was to create two distinct groups, but he avoided potential objections by allowing the sons of senators to wear the tunica – *laticlavia* - the exclusive tunic worn only by those of the senatorial class when they reached manhood, even though they were not yet actual members of the Senate.[6] Augustus created specific career paths for the sons of senators, known as the *cursus honorum*, usually involving being appointed to serve on the Committee of Twenty. This committee included those holding minor roles, such as *augurs*. This period was followed by service at a senior level in the legion, perhaps as a deputy commander.

Augustus also legislated for the marriage of sons of senators to the third generation as a distinct group. This had the effect of widening the numbers of those with senatorial rank and creating a

---

[5] Livy, *History of Rome*, XXI.63.
[6] Suetonius, *Augustus* 38.2.

distinction between serving senators and *senatorii*, those of senatorial rank.[7] If a senatorial family lost its senator, the whole family reverted to normal equestrian status. The numbers of those who were accorded equestrian status but who were not considered as full members of that class, rose under Augustus as he sought to use more and more equestrians in government positions that reported to and were responsible to him directly. This, in effect, created tiers within the equestrian class, ranging from those who were full members of the order to those whose status depended on their lineage.

Augustus' other major innovation with regard to the equestrian class was its organization along quasi-military lines. All equestrians were enrolled into one of six national cavalry squadrons called *turmae*. Each of these had a commander, and the six commanders formed a governing committee. To encourage the *equites* to identify themselves more closely with their peers, Augustus resurrected a defunct Republican practice called the inspection of the equites, *recognito equtum*, a ceremony involving all equites parading with their horses in front of the consuls every year.[8] Augustus cemented the separation of the senatorial class and the equites, including the sons of senators, by naming them *clarissimus*—most distinguished—and *egregious*—distinguished gentleman.[9] He also reserved a significant number of administrative posts exclusively for those of equestrian rank,[10] the most prestigious of which was the *praefectus Augusti* of Egypt. Similarly, the procurators Augusti, the chief financial officers of the imperial provinces, were also drawn exclusively from the ranks of the equestrians, and this post in Egypt was the aspiration of many.

After Augustus, equestrians took on even more of the administrative posts, including the Treasury and the directorship of grain supply.[11] As well as filling the key military post of Commander of the Praetorian Guard, equestrians also provided the *praefecti classis*, admirals of the Roman fleets at Misenum and Ravenna, and the Vigiles.[12] As the importance of the equestrians developed, they came to dominate Rome's law courts, providing judges and state secretaries. Hadrian exempted these post-holders from military service.[13] All of Augustus' innovations provided members of the equestrian order with ample opportunities to enrich themselves. The salaries of imperial prefects ranged from 15,000 denarii for smaller provinces to 75,000 per annum for Egypt. An equestrian *praefectus* of an auxiliary cohort was paid approximately 10,000 denarii per year, 50 times as much as a foot soldier and as much as two could earn in their entire enlistment.

---

[7] Roman Law Library (Lex Iulia de manitandis ordinibus).
[8] 'Equites', *Encyclopaedia Britannica* (2009).
[9] P. 8, *The Later Roman Empire* by A.H.M. Jones (1964). Oxford.
[10] P. 64, *The Complete Roman Army (The Complete Series)* by A. Goldsworthy (2003). Thames and Hudson: London.
[11] P. 65, *The Complete Roman Army (The Complete Series)* by A. Goldsworthy (2003). Thames and Hudson: London.
[12] P. 340, 'The Senate and Senatorial and Equestrian Posts' by R. Talbert. *Cambridge Ancient History Vol. X* (1996). Cambridge University Press.
[13] P. 8, *The Later Roman Empire* by A.H.M. Jones (1964). Oxford.

Inevitably, Augustus trusted and relied on this class far more than the senators. Augustus always saw senators as potential rivals, whereas equestrians were very much dependent on his good offices to maintain and advance themselves in the Roman world.[14] In due course, powerful equites came to be seen as threats in the same way as senators, explaining why Augustus, late in his reign, extended his ruling that senators could only visit Egypt with his express permission to equestrians, a policy retained by his successors.[15] Augustus' system proved to be extremely stable, and senators and equites cooperated in the smooth running of the empire until well into the 3rd century CE. The use of equestrians in the imperial service was crucial to Augustus and his vision of the Principate, and the fact that equestrians came to control such huge swathes of government, the economy and the military were the key to his success. Central to his ability to promote the equestrian class and retain its loyalty was his control of Egypt and its wealth.

The first Prefect appointed to Egypt was Cornelius Gallus, a close friend of Augustus who found one of his first tasks to be the suppression of an uprising in the Thebaid, the area surrounding the old capital of Thebes. He was successful and set up an inscription at Philae to record his achievements: "Gaius Cornelius Gallus son of Gnaeus, Roma eques, first prefect of Alexandria and Egypt after the overthrow of the kings by Caesar, son of a god, having been victorious in two pitched battles in the fifteen days within which he suppressed the revolt of the Thebans, capturing five cities, Boresis, Coptus, Ceramice, Diospolis Magna, and Ophieum and seizing the leaders of these revolts having led his army beyond the Nile cataract…dedicated this thank offering to his ancestral gods and to the Nile as his helpmate."[16]

---

[14] Tacitus, *Annals*, II 59.
[15] Tacitus, *Annals* II 59.
[16] CIL 3.14147, *Roman Civilization: Selected Readings, Vol. 2: The Empire* by N. Lewis and M. Reinhold (1990). Cambridge University Press.

An ancient bust of Cornelius Gallus

What is interesting is that the prefect made a dedication to his own family gods and the Nile, a sign of Augustus' policy of paying due honor and respect to local deities. He was, however, apparently prone to making exaggerated claims, and Augustus was not enamored of either his boasting or his forays into Sudan. He mysteriously committed suicide after being recalled to Rome.

Cornelius Gallus is best remembered today not for his limited political or military achievements, but his reputation as a poet, though very little of what he wrote has survived. In

1978, nine lines of his verse were discovered in Nubia, and this is now thought to be one of the oldest surviving examples of Latin poetry. Ovid rated him as the first of Rome's elegiac poets,[17] and he was held in the highest esteem by some of his contemporaries. One of his most famous contemporaries, Ovid, put him on a par with Virgil.[18]

The second prefect was Aelius Gallus who served two years, from 26-24 BCE. His rather unfortunate claim to fame rests with another disastrous expedition, on this occasion to Arabia. Augustus ordered the attempt to take Arabia under Roman control in the belief it was a repository of great hidden wealth.

Like his predecessor, this Gallus is also remembered for matters other than his military success. He is credited by Galen with discovering numerous medical remedies which, unfortunately, he had to utilize to the fullest during the campaign.[19] Aelius Gallus was a close friend of Strabo, and he provided detailed information about the attack on Arabia. Cassius Dio and Pliny the Elder also wrote about the expedition, and all concurred it had been an unmitigated disaster.[20] According to Strabo, Gallus' big mistake was relying too heavily on one Nabatean guide. Whether that was true or not, the net result was that the Roman force was almost entirely wiped out by a combination of thirst, disease, and military defeats. The Romans inherited small parts of Arabia when they had taken power in Egypt but even these were lost, and a disgruntled Augustus recalled his prefect to send another close friend, Gaius Petronius, to take over. Petronius does not seem to have learned much from the experiences of his predecessors, and he embarked on a foreign expedition himself. He invaded the kingdom of Kush but was not able to secure permanent gains. Instead, he razed the city of Napata to the ground and retreated to Egypt. The destruction of their capital and the enslavement of many of its citizens did not deter the Kushites from their raids into Roman territory. It was not until 22 BCE, when Petronius repulsed another Kushite raid, which they accepted client kingdom status. From then on, they became a lucrative trading partner.[21]

The prefects who followed were a relatively undistinguished group, none of whom experienced any major adventures or undertook revisions of the administrative system, ordered to secure maximum outcomes in terms of wealth and the maintenance of the grain supply that had become so vital to any emperor's hopes of a long reign. Romans never settled in Egypt in any great numbers, and as a result, civic life and culture remained largely Greek in the Roman period. Alexandria had become a major center for Jews who had fled from Judea for various reasons, and their abhorrence of what they had seen as the idolatry and paganism of both Greek and native religions led to direct conflict between the groups. The first major confrontation came during the reign of Caligula (34-41 CE). On this occasion, the Romans placed the blame squarely

---

[17] Ovid, *Tristia*, IV.
[18] Suetonius, *Augustus*, 66.
[19] Galen, II.
[20] Strabo, Geography, XVI; Cassius Dio, LIII, Pliny, *Natural History*, VI.32.
[21] P. 350 *The Nubian Past* by D.N. Edwards (2004). Routledge: London.

at the feet of the Jews and savagely put the riots down.

This pattern of the Romans supporting the Greeks against the Jews was repeated in all subsequent confrontations. After the destruction of Jerusalem in 70 CE, Alexandria, already home to a large Jewish population, became the main centre for Judaism in the Mediterranean world, and the religious conflicts between Greeks and Jews became commonplace, intense, and extremely violent. A major Jewish revolt erupted during Trajan's reign in 115 CE, bringing severe reprisals by the Romans against the Jewish community, including the loss of a number of privileges. The two-year insurrection came to be known as the Kitos War, but there is very little contemporary evidence or commentary about the episode. The uprising had come about due to increasing tensions between Jews and Greeks within Alexandria, and during the conflict, the Great Synagogue in the city was destroyed and thousands of Jews were massacred by the Romans.[22]

The result was that the vibrant Jewish community, which once numbered in excess of a quarter of a million people, was drastically reduced and never achieved anything like the status it had before the insurrection. However, while the traditional Jewish community's fortunes plummeted, a new sect born out of Judaism would begin to take hold in Egypt.

Christianity in Egypt

Christianity in Egypt dates to the very earliest years of the religion. Tradition assigns its introduction to Saint Mark 33 CE, though the Bishop of Caesarea, in his *History of the Early Church,* makes the claim that the introduction of Christianity to Egypt occurred a bit later, somewhere between 41 and 44 CE. There is debate as to whether Mark the Evangelist, who had founded the Coptic Church in Egypt, is the same as John Mark, cousin of Barnabas, but Hippolytus writes of them as distinct individuals who were both among the Seventy Disciples sent out by Christ to spread the gospel.

Mark is said to have composed his gospel based on accounts of Christ's life provided by the Apostle Peter, whom he had accompanied on his early travels. He left Peter to travel to Alexandria in the eighth year of Nero's reign, where he became the first Bishop of that city.[23]

The issue as to whether Mark, this first Bishop, actually wrote Saint Mark's Gospel is still a matter of scholarly debate, but his place as the founder of the Coptic Church in Egypt cannot be denied. The word "coptic" derives from the Greek word for Egypt, and the Coptic Church in Egypt is still very active, with followers numbering over 22 million with 18 million of them living in Egypt.

Today, Saint Mark's place as a central figure in Christianity is evident, and he is credited with,

---

[22] *The Ancient Jews from Alexander to Muhammad by S. Schwartz (2014). Cambridge University Press.*
[23] Eusebius, *Ecclesiastical History,* 2.14.6.

among other things, hosting the Last Supper and being present at the Marriage Feast at Caana. He is thought to have been born somewhere in North Africa, possibly Libya, and his African birth may have helped him in his missionary work in Egypt.

When he began his evangelical crusade, the Egyptians were still mostly loyal to the old gods, even after they came under Roman rule. While they made allowances for the state-sponsored worship of the emperor, they were as reluctant as their Hellenistic counterparts to countenance any acceptance of what they saw as another Jewish sect. According to Eusebius, the first convert to Christianity was a shoemaker named Anianus around 62 CE, and he went on to become the Patriarch of Alexandria after Saint Mark's martyrdom in 68 CE.

Initially, Christian converts came mainly from the Jewish community, but by the end of the 3rd century CE, almost all of the native Egyptian population had converted. The reasons for this very rapid rate of conversion have been the subject of speculation amongst historians for many years. The Egyptians, throughout their history, had been a very religiously-oriented people, as evidenced by their religious buildings and the symbiosis between everyday life and preparation for the afterlife. The Roman conquest subtly undermined Egyptian confidence in their religion, but the Roman concepts of religion were alien to their traditions and culture, whereas Christianity, on the other hand, contained many familiar and similar concepts, such as death and resurrection of a god, the judging of souls, and an afterlife that would be better than the present one for the true believers. Even the symbols had some similarities, with the shape of the Coptic cross and ankh, and the story of Mary and Joseph's flight to Egypt to escape Herod proved particularly powerful, as it proclaimed God had chosen Egypt as the safe haven for his infant son.

The transition to Christianity was not without its difficulties though, and the conflicts between Jews and followers of the polytheistic religions of Greece and Rome re-emerged in disputes between the latter and the new Christian groups. It was primarily to counter Hellenistic philosophy that the Alexandrian Church founded the Didascalia in the 2nd century A.D., which codified Christian philosophy and belief. It was this school that provided the core of Christian dogma and was the centre of intellectual debate regarding Church doctrines. Most of the early teachers and orators of the Church, such as Clement and Origen, were in the intellectual vanguard of the battle against polytheism and in the forefront of the missionary movement. Pantaenus, the founder of the Didascalia, was particularly successful in converting Egyptians and wrote extensively using the Greek alphabet to explain the new religion. The Didascalia was taught in Greek, and the teaching became accessible to virtually all elements of Egyptian society.

The greatest persecutions faced by Christians came, in the end, not from the local Hellenized population or native Egyptians but the Romans, and it was in Egypt that Christians were subjected to the greatest of this persecution. Unlike their Christian counterparts in Rome who had worshipped in catacombs and kept their religious beliefs secret whenever possible, the

Egyptian Christians were totally open from the start, building their churches in the most public spaces they could acquire. Diocletian was particularly savage in his persecution of Egyptian Christians. His brutality was so great that the Coptic Church dates itself from 264 CE, the year in which the greatest numbers of Christians were martyred in Egypt.[24]

G. Dallorto's picture of a bust of Diocletian

Roman attitudes to Christianity are known from a number of writers who expressed their views around the time of Trajan. From these works, it is clear the Roman view of Christianity was that it was depraved and "*superstitio*", a word applied to all cults or movements not officially sanctioned. Tacitus recorded that Domitian classified Christianity as a *superstitio Iudaica*,[25] which indicates much of the criticism against Christianity was based on earlier charges against Judaism, including the claim that both hated the human race. The refusal to swear allegiance to Roman gods and the emperor as a god marginalized Christians from the rest of society and was something the Roman authorities would not accept. In the specific case of Christianity, the Roman perception was that it encouraged sexual immorality and what they termed abominations, such as the eating and drinking of the blood of their god.[26]

---

[24] Eusebius, *Martyrs of Palestine; p.* 10, *Athanasius and Constantius: Theology and Politics in the Constantinian Empire* by T. Barnes (1993). Harvard University Press.
[25] Tacitus, *Annals*, XV.
[26] Tacitus, *Annals*, XV.

The most damning comments came from Pliny the Younger, who accused Christians of being obstinate despite the generous pardons offered to recant. Meanwhile, Suetonius, as with most Roman writers, didn't distinguish between the Christians and the Jews. He wrote that "since the Jews were continually involved in disturbances at the instigation of Christ, Emperor Claudius expelled them from Rome."[27] In his *Life of Nero*, he commented that Christians "were a set of men who adhered to a new and mischievous superstition."[28]

On the night of July 18th, 64 CE, the most significant event of Nero's time in power – and the one which, for better or for worse, would seal his name in infamy throughout the ages – took place. What became known as the Great Fire of Rome erupted sometime between the night of the 18th and the earliest hours of the 19th, and it consumed almost a quarter of the city while it burned out of control for five days. Interestingly, though there is archaeological evidence for the fact that the fire actually took place, and its extent was as significant as the sources seem to indicate, Tacitus is the only one who gives a comprehensive account of the fire, with other biographers not even mentioning it (aside from Pliny, who mentions it in connection to another incident). Yet the fire was definitely a momentous event, and one which would live on in history as Nero's worst hour.

The aftermath of the fire must have been a sight to behold. Much of Rome was a scorched and smoking ruin, and Nero was now faced with the unenviable task of trying to finance a rebuilding effort with state coffers that were already dangerously close to being empty. Part of his economic policy included the transportation of rubble from the blaze to nearby Ostia, where it was poured into the marshes both to get rid of it and to drain them of water, creating what eventually would become fertile farmland. Nero also ordered the reconstruction of the areas affected by the fire, having modern, evenly spaced and comfortable residences erected under his own supervision, and presumably employing many of those whose livelihoods were destroyed by the flames.

Nero capitalized on that unpopularity by accusing Christians of being responsible for the blaze, though it does not appear as though any motive was ever ascribed to them. Several were seized and, after being tortured, confessed (it is unclear whether they confessed to being Christians, or to the arson itself, but most sources are in accord in saying that they confessed *because* they were tortured). Scores of Christians were martyred, some draped in the skins of wild animals and then torn apart by dogs in the arena, others crucified in a mockery of Jesus's martyrdom, and still more were burned alive, nightly, to serve as illumination for Nero's garden banquets. The first institutionalized persecution of the Christians in the history of the Roman Empire (but not the last) had begun.

Tacitus described Nero's scapegoating of the Christians, writing, "Consequently, to get rid of the report, Nero fastened the guilt and inflicted the most exquisite tortures on a class hated for

---

[27] Suetonius, *Life of Claudius*, XXV.4.
[28] Suetonius, *Life of Nero*, XVI.

their abominations, called Christians by the populace. Christus, from whom the name had its origin, suffered the extreme penalty during the reign of Tiberius at the hands of one of our procurators, Pontius Pilatus, and a most mischievous superstition, thus checked for the moment, again broke out not only in Judaea, the first source of the evil, but even in Rome, where all things hideous and shameful from every part of the world find their centre and become popular. Accordingly, an arrest was first made of all who pleaded guilty; then, upon their information, an immense multitude was convicted, not so much of the crime of firing the city, as of hatred against mankind. Mockery of all sorts was added to their deaths. Covered with the skins of beasts, they were torn by dogs and perished, or were nailed to crosses, or were doomed to the flames and burnt, to serve as a nightly illumination, when daylight had expired."

Tacitus himself went on to describe Christianity as a "pernicious superstition," and he wrote that the Christians arrested for starting the fire had not been punished for that crime as much as for "their hatred [of] the human race. Besides being put to death they were made objects of amusement: they were clothed in the hides of beasts and torn to death by dogs. Others were crucified, others set on fire to illuminate the night after sunset."[29]

The persecution suffered by Egyptian Christians was possibly even more brutal than that suffered in other parts of the empire. Although the persecution reached its height under Diocletian, there were similarly savage repressions of Christians under Septimus Severus and Maximinus I. In Egypt, special equipment was developed to enhance the pain of those being tortured, and there are numerous examples of Christians being lashed, stoned, blinded, and castrated. From the Roman perspective, the torture was not a punishment so much as a device to make recalcitrant Christians recant and acknowledge Roman gods and the emperor. If they did so, they would be released, but if they did not, then the torture invariably resulted in death.

As is often the case, the deaths of so many martyrs had the opposite effect of the one the Romans intended, and each new martyr seemed to lead to more converts. In Egypt, Christianity came to be adopted as the people's religion, and the Church flourished and spread its influence throughout the Roman world.

One particular aspect of Christianity developed in Egypt with a great impact on later European history was monasticism. Saint Antony is generally credited with the foundation of the ascetic monastic life, and he is often referred to as Antony the Great or Antony the Abbot to distinguish him from a number of other Saints named Antony. He is also known as Father of All Monks. He was born in Egypt, and his life and work are relatively well-known thanks to *Life of St Anthony*, a biography written by Athanasius of Alexandria. He was brought up in Coma in Lower Egypt by wealthy parents, but after their death, when he was about 18, he renounced his worldly goods to follow Christ's injunction, selling all he had and giving to the poor so he could have "treasures in heaven."[30] He became an ascetic, living in and around his hometown for the next 15 years.

---

[29] Tacitus, *Annals*, XV.

Antony went even further in the next period of his life by retreating to the desert to live an essentially hermetic life. Although he was not the first of the ascetic hermits since there had been Pagan hermits before him, he took the concept to the extreme and located himself in the barren Nitrian Desert about 60 miles from Alexandria, where he remained for 13 years.[31]

Athanasius describes Antony's sufferings in the desert and the temptations he had to overcome through prayer. Having moved to live in a tomb, he was, it is claimed by his biographer, beaten mercilessly by the devil who resented his piety. His experiences in the tomb presumably prompted him to move on, and he spent the next 20 years even deeper in the desert, at a place named Pispir. There, he blocked himself into a cell and communicated only rarely with visitors through a small hole through which food was also passed.[32]

After his years of self-imposed incarceration, he emerged to help spread the gospel and bolster the Christian community which was, by that time, undergoing the worst of the Diocletian persecutions. He arrived in Alexandria in 311 CE, ignored warnings from the Romans, and began preaching. For whatever reason, he was not arrested, unlike so many of his followers, and when the persecutions ended, he returned to the desert. By then, however, his fame was so great that he was constantly beset by visitors seeking his counsel. Many of these visitors became his disciples, and he organized them into communities that spread throughout Egypt and the Roman world.[33] One disciple, Macarius the Great, carried on his work, providing the key elements of monasticism Saint Benedict had used in the development of his Rule 200 years later.

Antony's sayings and those of his major disciples were incorporated into the *Sayings of the Desert Fathers*, which profoundly influenced Christian thinking. It is said that Emperor Constantine wrote to Antony personally asking for his advice. Toward the end of his life, he returned to Alexandria to lead the opposition to the Arian heresy.[34]

Antony's influence on the early Church cannot be overestimated. He played a major role not only in promoting the concept of monasticism but in consolidating Christianity in Egypt, and through his disciples and personal influence, the whole Roman Empire.

Another Egyptian who played a significant part in the development of coenobitic or communal monasticism was Saint Pachomius. Born in Upper Egypt, he was conscripted into the Roman auxiliaries where he met Coptic Christians and converted. He became a follower of Antony and withdrew into the desert near Thebes around 314 CE. Pachomius had a talent for administration and was soon involved in building monastic enclosures where the scattered monks could live in communities. He drew up routines for the monks that balanced work and prayer and his

---

[30] Eusebius, 1878.
[31] *Butler's Lives of the Saints edited by* M. Walsh (1991). Harper Collins.
[32] Athanasius, *Life of St. Anthony*.
[33] Eusebius, 1878.
[34] *The Story of Christianity: Volume 1* by J. Gonzalez (1984). Harper Collins.

monasteries, with their hierarchical structures, became models for those that came later. Pachomius' life was recorded by Palladius in his *Lausiac History*. One specific legacy among many was that he was known by the title Abba, meaning father, which became the title Abbot and was used by leaders of subsequent monasteries. He founded 11 monasteries, but many more were founded throughout Egypt, the Middle East, and later Western Europe.[35]

Egypt and the Politics of the Empire

Given Egypt's pivotal position within the empire, it is no surprise it was embroiled in complex political battles for the ultimate control of Rome. No one unable to control Egypt could aspire to rule the empire for long. In 139 A.D., native Egyptians, led by Isidorus, rose in rebellion in what became known as the Bucolic War. The insurrection was put down by Avidius Cassius after several years of fighting, after which he declared himself emperor in 175 A.D. Marcus Aurelius was despatched to deal with the usurper, and Cassius was defeated. A similar train of events occurred in 193 A.D. when Pescennius Niger was proclaimed emperor in Egypt; he, too, was defeated.

Caracalla was responsible for the next major changes in Egyptian social structure when he gave Roman citizenship to all Egyptians, though it is more likely he did so to extort additional taxes rather than as a notion of fairness.[36] The economic resources Egypt provided did not change to any great extent in the Roman era as compared to the Ptolemaic period, but what did change was the efficiency with which the wealth was extracted through ever more sophisticated taxation systems. Assessments were made of the value of land, and taxes were paid in kind. In addition, smaller taxes were levied through custom duties on a variety of goods.

The grain exported to Rome, however, always remained the key issue, and securing an uninterrupted supply was the primary objective of every prefect. They also took the opportunity to increase their wealth, and in doing so, helped benefit the general economic well-being of the province.

Successive prefects encouraged the purchase of land and promoted private enterprises in commerce, manufacturing, and trade through reduced taxation rates. The poor, on the other hand, had to scratch a living from the land they'd rented from the state or private landlords and bore the brunt of the taxation system. Egyptian economy was complex, and even at the local level, the use of coinage was commonplace. The net result was that Egypt economically thrived from the reign of Nero, and was at the height of its economic power by the end of the 2nd century CE.

By the end of the 3rd century CE, the debasement of the currency began to have a negative impact on Egypt's economic situation.[37] The economy degenerated to such an extent that

---

[35] Pp. 73-76, *Pachomius: The Making of a Community in Fourth Century Egypt* by P. Rousseau (1985). University of California Press.
[36] Provided for under the statutes of the *Constitution of Antoninus*.

Diocletian and Constantine enacted drastic reforms that played a part in the empire's split, and Egypt became a part of the eastern half.

It is probably true to say there is no one overarching reason for the emergence of two separate, imperial entities following the split of the empire into east and west. Some writers highlight the problems created by the vast size of the empire, which encompassed over two million square miles at its height and spanned over three continents, resulting in significant problems in communication and making governance difficult. It is certainly true that the empire was enormous and communication between Rome and its furthest reaches could involve months of travel. In such circumstances, it was relatively easy for local figures to ignore or modify Roman dictates or to operate semi-autonomously.

Other academics point to underlying economic issues confronting the empire. It has been suggested that the western part was essentially consumer and debtor, and the eastern part the provider of wealth and food. In this context, Egypt was vital, particularly in relation to the provision of grain. The western part of the empire was much poorer and more rural than the east, but despite this rural nature, the real wealth of the empire lay in agriculture from the African continent, particularly Egypt. This is what kept Italy from starvation. The underlying economic weakness of the western empire was masked by the wealth of the eastern. These economic imbalances contributed to the instability in the empire in the 3rd century A.D., leading to Diocletian's attempt to impose far-reaching, centralized control on the economy as a means of protecting the empire's integrity.

He instituted price controls by forcing workers into hereditary professions, but punitive taxation fomented dissatisfaction so he had to create more reasons to find ways around the system. In rural areas, the net result was less tax revenue, not more, as local aristocrats conspired with the rural population to avoid taxation. In the urbanized and populous east, it was much harder to evade taxation, resulting in the growth of a highly bureaucratic, hierarchical administrative structure. Unlike rural areas in the west, the aristocrats of the east became the bureaucracy. This only added to the growing cultural gulf between the two parts of the empire already manifesting itself through things like the west speaking Latin while the east spoke Greek. Diocletian then took a step preparing the way for the split by dividing the empire into four administrative regions in an attempt to make it more manageable. These reforms could not mask the simple truth that the west faced a situation in which food prices were high and rising, as well as a huge deficit with nothing to offer in exchange for the goods it imported from the east. To address the issue, the coinage was debased, but this led to further inflation, instability, and imbalance.

Apart from these economic problems and those associated with the difficulties of efficiently administering such a vast territory, some writers have concluded the real reason for the division

---

[37] *Coinage in Roman Egypt* by E. Christiansen (2004). Aarhus University Press.

lay in the fact the empire was fundamentally rotten at its core. By this, they mean that the system set up by Augustus and his successors had some superficial success in its early years in terms of securing the power of the emperor, but that maintenance of power was purely based on military might. By creating a more mobile class system, the way was opened for a wider selection of people to aspire to power, when what was actually needed was the ability to control military forces. Things eventually started coming to a head in the 3rd century.[38]

On a more positive note, Diocletian's administrative reforms also involved a restructuring of the systems in Egypt which proved helpful in securing Egypt's continued prosperity once the empire finally split. These systems were built upon by Constantine once he took complete control of the empire. The province was divided into four administrative areas, each of which had further subdivisions to create smaller units that were more easily managed. The reforms also involved the splitting of a number of official posts and the creation of separate military and civil officials, known as the *praeses* and the *dux*. For the first time, the whole province was also placed under the overall supervision of the most senior official in Antioch. Constantine consolidated these reforms in Egypt, and they proved vital in ensuring Egypt remained as the most important exporter of food in the ancient world.

Diocletian's answer to Rome's problems was the introduction of a system of devolution, known as the Tetrarchy, in 293. The word itself comes from the Greek, meaning leadership of the people by four. The Tetrarchy lasted until 313, when the four became two. Shortly after that, under Constantine, the system ended when he assumed sole rule. The Tetrarchs were made up of two co-emperors and two Caesars, or junior emperors, each ruling from their own capital. None were based in Rome, as it was felt that each should be based on the borders of states with actual or potential enemies. Thus, the empire was ruled by Nicodemia in Asia Minor, Trier in Germany, Sirmium in modern-day Serbia, and Mediolanum in northern Italy. Rome remained the nominal capital of the empire under its own prefect.

Diocletian's reforms ultimately failed, and his pathological hatred of Christians contributed to the highly volatile situation, but it could still be argued that his policies served to keep the empire together in some sense. The consolidation of division was always likely to cause difficulties.

It was into this very unsettled scenario that Constantine, known historically as Constantine the Great, emerged. Rome was engulfed in another civil war in the early 4th century, and according to both Eusebius and Lactantius, two of Constantine's principal biographers, the day before the Battle of the Milvian Bridge, Constantine was stricken by a vision. Lactantius claims that Constantine was visited by an angel as he dreamt the night before battle, while Eusebius's version is even more theatrical. According to Eusebius, while Constantine's army was on the march, a fiery symbol, shaped like the crossed X and P of the Latin Alphabet (☧) and bearing beneath it the legend "Ἐν Τούτῳ Νίκα" ("by this sign, you will conquer"), appeared in the sky

---

[38] *Rome and its Emperors A.D 193-284 A.D* by O. Hekstedt (2008). Edinburgh.

above. The X and P represented the Greek letters Xhi and Rho, the first two letters of Christ's name in the Greek spelling.

Jean-Christophe Benoist's picture of a bust of Constantine

Presumably, such a divine manifestation would have prompted an on-the-spot conversion, and Constantine certainly alluded to that in later propaganda, but there is significant evidence that the original manifestation was actually viewed as a pagan divine revelation. In that version, the revelation was interpreted as being the halo of *Sol Invictus,* the Sun God with whom Constantine claimed a long-standing association and whose iconography was depicted in coins issued by Constantine even years after the battle.

This gold coin, minted in 313, depicts Constantine with *Sol Invictus*.

One problem with the theory that Constantine merely observed what he thought was a divine revelation from *Sol Invictus* is that accounts agree he changed the appearance of his equipment before the battle. Some scholars have rather optimistically suggested that the fiery symbol was in fact a sun dog, but whatever the source of Constantine's divine inspiration, whether miraculous, scientific or simply clever propaganda, on the day of battle his armies apparently approached Maxentius's forces with the Xhi Rho painted on their shields. According to Eusebius: "Assuming therefore the Supreme God as his patron, and invoking His Christ to be his preserver and aid, and setting the victorious trophy, the salutary symbol, in front of his soldiers and body-guard, he marched with his whole forces, trying to obtain again for the Romans the freedom they had inherited from their ancestors."

Having consolidated his position within his own domains, Constantine then set about securing his borders from invasion. Matters outside the Western Roman Empire were still on a knife's edge with Maximin and Licinius at each other's throats, and so to smooth matters over Constantine suggested that he and Licinius meet in Mediolanum and talk peace. Accordingly, the two Emperors met in the city in 313, with Constantine asking that Licinius make good on his previous promise to marry his sister Constantia.

However, the most famous and significant result of the encounter was not the renewal of their alliance but their joint edict, later dubbed the Edict of Milan, on religious freedom. The Edict of Milan was not quite the landmark that Christian scholars declared it to be, given that Galerius had issued a similar edict shortly before his death. In Galerius's edict in 311, Christians who "followed such a caprice and had fallen into such a folly that they would not obey the institutes of antiquity" were excused from their "errors": "Wherefore, for this our indulgence, they ought to pray to their God for our safety, for that of the republic, and for their own, that the commonwealth may continue uninjured on every side, and that they may be able to live securely in their homes."

With that said, the Edict of Milan certainly went further than Galerius did, by declaring all religions exempt from persecution and proclaiming freedom of worship for all, with a special emphasis on Christianity. Not only were Christians freed from any persecution and allowed to worship in peace, but their property (including entire churches) and wealth that had previously been seized in various religious purges over the years were granted to them with full restitution.

Affairs within the Church did not immediately begin to run smoothly though. Even before the threat of persecution had been removed, the Christians were divided by a series of internal disputes, particularly virulent in Alexandria. The basis of the conflict was the disagreement among Christians regarding the doctrines of Arius, known as Arianism. Arius was an Alexandrian who had propounded a non-Trinitarian doctrine relating to the nature of Christ.[39] He asserted that Christ was the Son of God who had come into existence at a specific point in time created by God the Father and so was separate from the Father and subservient to him.[40] These views were very different from beliefs held by many Christians, known as Homoousian, who contended that Christ had always existed and was equal to the Father. The two sides argued long and hard in the School in Alexandria, even though, initially, the two doctrines had co-existed side-by-side. Both were considered orthodox, but conflicts developed as each side tried to win converts to its interpretation.

The disagreements continued until Constantine finally took control of the empire and Homoousianism was adopted as the official doctrine at the Council of Nicaea in 325 A.D. At that council, Arianism was declared heretical, and the Nicene Creed adopted as the summary of Christian beliefs. Of the 300 bishops at the council, only two did not endorse the Creed condemning Arianism.[41] Constantine imposed the death penalty on those who refused to hand over Arian texts: "If any writing by Arius should be found it should be handed over to the flames, so that not only will the wickedness of his teachings be obliterated but nothing will be left to remind anyone of him. I hereby make a public order that if someone should be discovered to have hidden a writing composed by Arian and not to have immediately brought it forward and destroyed it by fire his penalty shall be death."[42]

---

[39] 'Arianism', *Encyclopaedia Britannica* (2009).
[40] 'Arianism', *Encyclopaedia Britannica* (2009).
[41] 'Nicaea, Council of', *Encyclopaedia Britannica* (2009).

It is a fairly safe assumption that most Christians did not understand the issue in dispute.[43] The matter resolved at Nicaea was thrown into confusion again when the First Synod of Tyre declared Arius was not a heretic after all in 335 A.D.,[44] and Constantine was baptised by Arian Bishop Eusebius.[45] Later councils re-imposed the ban on Arianism, but in the period up to Constantine's death, the dispute proved extremely divisive and caused a very real disruption in the Egyptian cities that had given rise to these so-called heresies.

Nevertheless, despite this favoritism towards Christianity, there is still no definitive proof that Constantine was a Christian at this stage. Indeed, two years later, when he erected the famous Arch of Constantine, he made sacrifices to Victory and other deities. Though there are religious motifs on the Arch itself, and in the way it was constructed and sited, they are all pagan. There is no Christian iconography to be found anywhere on the arch.

In his time, Constantine affected nearly every conceivable cultural aspect of the Roman Empire, most notably in its religion but also even in attire and appearance. Constantine revived the clean shaven look, which Augustus himself had favored 300 years earlier. Given his conversion of the empire and relocation to Constantinople, Constantine directly shaped the histories of Europe, the Byzantine Empire, the Roman Empire, and the growth of the Catholic

---

[42] Athanasius, *Life of Constantine*, 18.
[43] p.267, *Church History Vol. I: From Christ to the Pre-Reformation* by E. Ferguson (2013). Zondervan.
[44] Socrates of Constantinople, *Church History*, I.33.
[45] *The Story of Christianity: Volume 1* by J. Gonzalez (1984). Harper Collins.

Church. While he was being venerated as a saint by the Eastern Orthodox Christians in the Byzantine Empire, Charlemagne was claiming his mantle in Western Europe about 400 years later, making sure that his own court was adorned with monuments to Constantine. Constantine's popularity even extended to Britain, where 12th century Britons were trying to claim him as a native son by claiming Helena actually originated from Colchester. To this day, Constantine's name has remained popular and in use.

At the same time, Constantine was shaped by his times just as much as he shaped them. His decision to regard Rome an unsalvageable Imperial capital was the consequence of a deeply rooted pragmatism; after all, Constantine himself had conquered Rome. It may also be argued that his conversion and successive edict of religious tolerance were also politically pragmatic. The traditional Roman religious worship, which had endured for hundreds of years, had begun to be supplanted by a new wave of "mystery cults", secretive sects with obscure rituals which had gained enormous popularity. The most popular of these, of course, was Christianity, whose adherents had forgone the traditional initiation mysteries which made each separate cult an elitist affair and opened it to all as a populist religion. Christianity was no longer an obscure sect whose members inspired fear and could thus be conveniently scapegoats for tragedies like the great fire of Rome. In the 1st century, they could be persecuted and even slaughtered with relative, but by Constantine's time, they had become a burgeoning and powerful religious force whose faithful could cause serious political problems if they were not appeased. By proclaiming himself a Christian and publishing his edict of religious tolerance, Constantine was pragmatically acknowledging that Christianity was, or was fast becoming, the dominant religious group in the Empire.

Constantinople, Constantine's "new" city, was founded in 324, dedicated in 330, and renamed Constantinople almost immediately after Constantine's victory over Licinius. The dedication ceremonies included both Pagan and Christian rites, but in this "new Rome," Pagan temples and cults were conspicuous by their absence.[46] The reunification of the empire, albeit not particularly long-lived, allowed Constantine to complete many of Diocletian's reforms, as well as allow him to introduce innovations of his own. His major reforms included the creation of a new field army and military positions that reported directly to the emperor. This extended the principle initiated by Diocletian of separating civil and military functions in the administration of provinces and was particularly relevant to the governance of Egypt.

Once he had decided to live more or less permanently in the Christianized east, Constantine promoted Christianity more aggressively. He openly rejected Paganism, though he never persecuted them. He promoted Christians into new posts and welcomed bishops to his court.[47] Constantine's patronage was a decisive turning point in the history of the Church as he supported it financially and had a large number of basilicas built, exempted Christians from some taxes,

---

[46] P. 508, *The Oxford Dictionary of Byzantium* edited by A. Kazhdan (1991). Oxford University Press.
[47] It was he that summoned the First Ecumenical Council at Nicaea in 325 A.D. mentioned above.

and returned property that had been seized by Diocletian as well as land granted to the Church.[48] The architecture of his new city was overtly Christian, and churches were built inside the city walls, a very visible illustration of the religion's status. No Pagan temples were built, and as there were no pre-existing ones, Paganism was not represented in the city.[49] Significantly, Constantine made non-Christians contribute to the building of Christian churches.

Constantine increasingly employed Christians in senior positions, but he never stopped utilizing the non-Christian aristocratic elites, and right up until his death, approximately two-thirds of senior positions were held by Pagans. He did change laws to bring them more in line with his Christian leanings, though. For example, in deference to Christian piety and sensibilities, he abolished crucifixion, replacing it with hanging. He was also responsible for making Sunday, a day sacred to both Christians and followers of Sol Invictus, an official day of rest. Markets were forbidden, and public buildings closed on that day, though agricultural work was allowed.[50] Other changes also reflected his Christian leanings; for example, a prisoner could be branded on his feet but not on his face, which was deemed to have been made in God's image. Gladiatorial games were also abolished.[51]

A particularly important order given directly by Constantine to Bishop Eusebius was that 50 Bibles be produced for the Church of Constantinople. Athanasius wrote that 340 Alexandrian scribes were employed to fulfill the commission.[52] These Bibles, along with the Codex Alexandrinus, are the earliest extant Christian Bibles, which testifies to the importance of the Egyptian Church in the spread of Christianity within the empire.[53] Though Constantine never made Christianity the official state religion of the empire, he did pave the way for that to happen in 380 A.D. His policies established the precedent for having a Christian emperor in the Church. What emerged was that the bishops took responsibility for doctrine, but the emperor had the responsibility for maintaining orthodoxy and rooting out heretics. In the later years of his reign, he ordered the destruction of Pagan temples, reversing his earlier, more tolerant approach to the older religions.[54]

Constantine believed he had a greater chance of salvation if he waited until he was dying before being baptized. He died in May 337, leaving his son, Constantius II, an Arian, to take over in the east. He received Egypt, while his half-brother, Constantine, was left the western half, restoring the position that had existed under the Tetrarchy.

As far as it is known, Constantine never visited Egypt himself, but his influence on its history

---

[48] *Christianizing the Roman Empire A.D. 100-400 A.D.* by R. MacMullen (1984). Yale University Press.
[49] P. 55, *Medieval Worlds* by R. Gerberding and J.H. Moran Cruz (2004). New York.
[50] *New Catholic Encyclopaedia* (1908); *Christianizing the Roman Empire A.D. 100-400 A.D.* by R. MacMullen (1984). Yale University Press.
[51] P. 700, *The Word Made Flesh: A History of Christian Thought* by M.R. Miles (2004). Blackwell.
[52] Ath. Apol. Const. 4.
[53] P. 414, *The Canon Debate* edited by L.M. McDonald & J.A. Sanders (2002). Hendrikson Publishers.
[54] P. 14, *The Popes and the Papacy in the Early Middle Ages* by J. Richards (1979). Routledge & Kegan.

was immense. If the early Christian writers are to be believed, Egyptian Christians, such as Saint Antony, were highly significant in persuading him to treat Christianity with much greater tolerance than his immediate predecessor, and in his final deathbed conversion.

Perhaps most importantly, while Constantine's reunification of the empire under his rule proved short-lived and the split after his death became permanent, historians still point to the fact he secured the Roman Empire, at least in the east, for another 1,000 years. In that sense, he also irrevocably linked Egypt to the Byzantine Empire, rather than with Western Europe, and Egypt's wealth and fertility guaranteed it would remain an important part of the Byzantine Empire throughout the Middle Ages.

Online Resources

Other books about Egypt by Charles River Editors

Other books about ancient history by Charles River Editors

Bibliography

Arrian. 1971. *The Campaigns of Alexander*. Translated by Aubrey de Sélincourt. London: Penguin Books.

Bowman, Alan K. 1996. *Egypt after the Pharaohs: 332 BC-AD 642 from Alexander to the Arab Conquest*. Los Angeles: University of California Press.

Bryce, Trevor. 2014. *Ancient Syria: A Three Thousand Year History*. Oxford: Oxford University Press.

Caesar, Julius. 2006. *The Civil Wars*. Translated by A.G. Peskett. Cambridge, Massachusetts: Harvard University Press.

Cassius Dio. 1954. *Roman History*. Translated by Earnest Cary. Cambridge, Massachusetts: Harvard University Press.

Casson, Lionel. 2001. *Libraries in the Ancient World*. New Haven, Connecticut: Yale University Press.

Chauveau, Michael. *Egypt in the Age of Cleopatra: History and Society under the Ptolemies*. Translated by David Lorton. Ithaca, New York: Cornell University Press, 2000.

Diodorus Siculus. 2004. *The Library of History*. Translated by C.H. Oldfather. Cambridge, Massachusetts: Harvard University Press.

Heller-Roazen, Daniel. 2002. "Tradition's Destruction: On the Library of Alexandria." *October Magazine* 100: 133-153.

Lloyd, Alan B. 2000. "The Ptolemaic Period (332-30 BC)." In *The Oxford History of Ancient Egypt*, edited by Ian Shaw, 395-421. Oxford: Oxford University Press.

Manetho. 2004. *Aegyptiaca.* Translated by W. G. Waddell. Cambridge, Massachusetts: Harvard University Press.

Plutarch. 1968. *Lives.* Edited and translated by Bernadotte Perrin. Cambridge, Massachusetts: Harvard University Press.

Polybius. 1960. *The Histories.* Translated by W.R. Paton. Cambridge, Massachusetts: Harvard University Press.

Price, Simon. 2001. "The History of the Hellenistic Period." In *The Oxford History of Greece and the Hellenistic World*, edited by John Boardman, Jasper Griffin, and Oswyn Murray, 364-389. Oxford: Oxford University Press.

Runia, David T. 1989. "Polis and Megalopolis: Philo and the Founding of Alexandria." *Mnemosyne* 42: 398-412.

Scheidel, Walter. 2004. "Creating a Metropolis: A Comparative Demographic Perspective." In *Ancient Alexandria between Egypt and Greece*, edited by W.V. Harris and Giovanni Ruffini, 1-32. Leiden: Brill.

Shaw, Ian and Paul Nicholson. 1995. *The Dictionary of Ancient Egypt*. New York: Harry N. Abrams.

Strabo. 2001. *Geography*. Translated by Horace Leonard Jones. Cambridge, Massachusetts: Harvard University Press.

Verbrugghe, Gerald P. and John M. Wickersham. 2001. *Berossos and Manetho, Introduced and Translated: Native traditions in Ancient Mesopotamia and Egypt*. Ann Arbor: University of Michigan Press.

Free Books by Charles River Editors

We have brand new titles available for free most days of the week. To see which of our titles are currently free, click on this link.

Discounted Books by Charles River Editors

We have titles at a discount price of just 99 cents everyday. To see which of our titles are currently 99 cents, click on this link.

Manufactured by Amazon.ca
Bolton, ON